はしがき

　本書『Active　Practical Reading 導入編』は，大学入学共通テスト，英検®，GTEC®に対応した速読問題集です。近年のリーディングの問題では，大意把握や情報検索といった速読の力がますます重要になってきています。そのため本書では，与えられた英文から必要な情報を短時間で見つけ出す「スキャニング（探し読み）」の技能を，"Practice makes perfect!"(習うより慣れよ。)を実践しながら身につけることができるように構成しました。各レッスンで用意した実用的で多様な英文と設問を通して，本書がみなさんの大学入試に向けた英語学習に役立つことを期待しています。

【本書の構成と利用法】

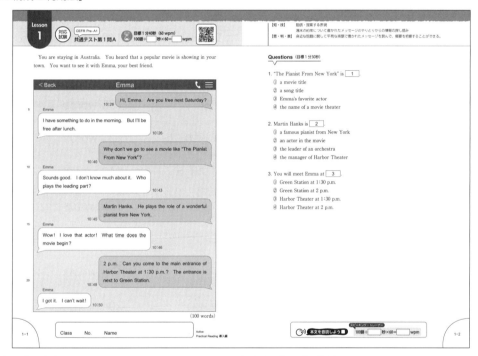

●左ページ：本文

・各試験の英文形式に対応した本文です。

・本書ではレッスンが進むにつれて，1分あたりに読むべき語数(wpm)がだんだん多くなるように目標時間を設定しています。上部(👤)の計算式を使って，読みの速度を算出してみましょう。

・二次元コードを読み取って，本文の音声をPCやスマートフォンから聞くことができます。(英文形式によって，一部の音声が収録されていないレッスンがあります。)

●右ページ：設問

・各試験の設問形式に対応した設問です。(設問数は異なります。)

・求められる「知識・技能」と「思考力・判断力・表現力」をページ上部(【知・技】【思・判・表】)に示しました。

・スピーキング・トレーナーを使って，本文の音読練習をすることができます。下部の計算式を使って，1分あたりに音読できた語数(wpm)を算出してみましょう。

CONTENTS

Lesson	対応試験		テキストタイプ	本文語数	目標 wpm	
1	共通テスト	第1問A	メッセージ	100 words	60 wpm	
2	共通テスト	第1問A	SNS	107 words	60 wpm	
3	英検®3級	第3部A	広告	104 words	60 wpm	
4	共通テスト	第1問A	告知記事	99 words	60 wpm	
5	GTEC®	パートB	説明文	101 words	60 wpm	
6	英検®3級	第3部A	掲示	133 words	65 wpm	
7	GTEC®	パートB	ウェブサイト	148 words	65 wpm	
8	GTEC®	パートB	説明文	154 words	70 wpm	
9	共通テスト	第1問A	新聞記事	150 words	70 wpm	
10	共通テスト	第2問A	レビューサイト	135 words	75 wpm	
11	GTEC®	パートB	ウェブサイト	142 words	75 wpm	
12	英検®3級	第3部B	メール	152 words	75 wpm	
13	共通テスト	第2問A	レシピ	156 words	80 wpm	
14	GTEC®	パートB	広告	173 words	80 wpm	
15	英検®3級	第3部B	メール	204 words	85 wpm	
16	共通テスト	第2問A	旅程表	239 words	85 wpm	
17	共通テスト	第3問A	ブログ記事	206 words	90 wpm	
18	GTEC® 英検®3級	パートC 第3部C	説明文	205 words	90 wpm	
19	オリジナル問題		ブログ記事	231 words	90 wpm	
20	GTEC® 英検®3級	パートC 第3部C	説明文	225 words	90 wpm	
21	オリジナル問題		ブログ記事	254 words	90 wpm	
22	GTEC® 英検®3級	パートC 第3部C	説明文	250 words	90 wpm	

求められる資質・能力	
知識・技能	思考力・判断力・表現力
□勧誘・提案する表現／□週末の約束について書かれたメッセージのやりとりからの情報の探し読み	□身近な話題に関して平易な英語で書かれたメッセージを読んで，概要を把握することができる。
□賛成する表現・理由を述べる表現／□電子書籍について書かれた SNS からの情報の探し読み	□身近な話題に関して平易な英語で書かれた SNS の投稿を読んで，概要を把握することができる。
□金額を表す表現／□セールについて書かれた広告からの情報の探し読み	□日常生活に関連した身近な広告から，自分が必要とする情報を読み取ることができる。
□予定を表す表現／□スピーチコンテストについて書かれた告知記事からの情報の探し読み	□日常生活に関連した記事から，自分が必要とする情報を読み取ることができる。
□自然環境を表す表現／□ハワイについて書かれた説明文からの情報の探し読み	□平易な英語で書かれたごく短い説明を読んで，概要を把握することができる。
□高校の一般公開日について書かれた掲示からの情報の探し読み	□日常生活に関連した身近な掲示から，自分が必要とする情報を読み取ることができる。
□駐輪場の空き状況について書かれたウェブサイトからの情報の探し読み	□日常生活に関連した身近なウェブサイトから，自分が必要とする情報を読み取ることができる。
□スポーツに関する表現／□クリケットについて書かれた説明文からの情報の探し読み	□平易な英語で書かれたごく短い説明を読んで，概要を把握することができる。
□病気に関する表現／□マラリアの予防について書かれた新聞記事からの情報の探し読み	□日常生活に関連した記事から，自分が必要とする情報を読み取ることができる。
□評価する表現／□ホテルについてのレビューサイトからの情報の探し読み	□身の回りの事柄に関して平易な英語で書かれたごく短い説明を読んで，イラストを参考にしながら，概要や要点を捉えたり，推測したり，情報を事実と意見に整理することができる。
□バスツアーの内容について書かれたウェブサイトからの情報の探し読み	□日常生活に関連した身近なウェブサイトから，自分が必要とする情報を読み取ることができる。
□誘う表現／□花見の誘いについてのメールのやりとりからの情報の探し読み	□平易な英語で書かれたごく短いメールのやりとりを読んで，概要を把握することができる。
□料理方法や数量に関する表現／□料理方法が書かれたレシピからの情報の探し読み	□平易な英語で書かれたレシピを読んで，イラストなどを参考にしながら，概要や要点をとらえたり，推測したり，情報を事実と意見に整理することができる。
□時間や手順を説明する表現／□水族館のイベントについて書かれた広告からの情報の探し読み	□日常生活に関連した身近な広告から，自分が必要とする情報を読み取ることができる。
□自分のことを紹介する表現／□ホストファミリーとのメールのやりとりからの情報の探し読み	□平易な英語で書かれたごく短いメールのやりとりを読んで，概要を把握することができる。
□日程を描写する表現／□旅程表からの情報の探し読み	□平易な英語で書かれた旅程表を読んで，イラストなどを参考にしながら，概要や要点をとらえたり，推測したり，情報を事実と意見に整理することができる。
□過去の出来事を描写する表現／□図書館での出来事について書かれたブログ記事からの情報の探し読み	□平易な英語で書かれたごく短い物語を読んで，イラストなどを参考にしながら，概要を把握することができる。
□犬と人間の関係について書かれた説明文からの情報の探し読み	□身近な話題に関して平易な英語で書かれた短い説明を読んで，概要を把握することができる。
□対照する表現／□24時間営業について書かれたブログ記事からの情報の探し読み	□平易な英語で書かれたごく短い物語を読んで，イラストなどを参考にしながら，概要を把握することができる。
□時間的順序を表す表現／□消しゴムの歴史について書かれた説明文からの情報の探し読み	□身近な話題に関して平易な英語で書かれた短い説明を読んで，概要を把握することができる。
□季節の好き嫌いについて書かれたブログ記事からの情報の探し読み	□平易な英語で書かれたごく短い物語を読んで，イラストなどを参考にしながら，概要を把握することができる。
□言語に関する表現／□フランス語について書かれた説明文からの情報の探し読み	□身近な話題に関して平易な英語で書かれた短い説明を読んで，概要を把握することができる。

Lesson 1

対応試験

CEFR Pre-A1

共通テスト第1問A

目標 1 分40秒 （60 wpm）
100語÷□秒×60=□ wpm

You are staying in Australia. You heard that a popular movie is showing in your town. You want to see it with Emma, your best friend.

< Back   Emma   📞 ☰

> Hi, Emma. Are you free next Saturday?
> 10:26

5   Emma

> I have something to do in the morning. But I'll be free after lunch.
> 10:26

> Why don't we go to see a movie like "The Pianist From New York"?
> 10:40

10   Emma

> Sounds good. I don't know much about it. Who plays the leading part?
> 10:43

> Martin Hanks. He plays the role of a wonderful pianist from New York.
> 10:45

15   Emma

> Wow! I love that actor! What time does the movie begin?
> 10:46

> 2 p.m. Can you come to the main entrance of Harbor Theater at 1:30 p.m.? The entrance is next to Green Station.
> 10:49

20   Emma

> I got it. I can't wait!
> 10:50

(100 words)

Class   No.   Name

Active
Practical Reading 導入編

Questions （目標１分30秒）

1. "The Pianist From New York" is ┌─ 1 ─┐ .
   ① a movie title
   ② a song title
   ③ Emma's favorite actor
   ④ the name of a movie theater

2. Martin Hanks is ┌─ 2 ─┐ .
   ① a famous pianist from New York
   ② an actor in the movie
   ③ the leader of an orchestra
   ④ the manager of Harbor Theater

3. You will meet Emma at ┌─ 3 ─┐ .
   ① Green Station at 1:30 p.m.
   ② Green Station at 2 p.m.
   ③ Harbor Theater at 1:30 p.m.
   ④ Harbor Theater at 2 p.m.

Lesson 2

対応試験

CEFR Pre-A1

共通テスト第1問A

目標 1 分50秒 (60 wpm)
107語÷☐秒×60=☐wpm

You like reading books.　You have found some interesting posts on an SNS.

 Tim@Tim0104

E-books are really nice!　You can always read your favorite books at any place on your smartphone.　You can't do that with printed books.　I want to hear your
5　opinion, too.

20：40　10/20

 Chloe@life_design_C
@Tim0104

I agree with you.　I always carry hundreds of books in my smartphone.
10　They are not heavy at all!　That's amazing!

7：40　10/21

 Takashi@Steven_8
@Tim0104

It's nice to be able to keep many books in one device.　But I like printed
15　books better because it is said that we can't take notes on the pages in
e-books.　Also, I don't like looking at a display for a long time.

8：05　10/21

(107 words)

Class　　　No.　　　Name

Active
Practical Reading 導入編

Questions （目標 1 分30秒）

1. Tim wants people to ☐ 1 ☐ .

　① agree with him

　② give up reading printed books

　③ read their favorite books

　④ share their ideas about e-books

2. Chloe writes that she ☐ 2 ☐ .

　① carries a lot of e-books

　② carries a lot of printed books

　③ likes reading heavy books

　④ likes reading light books

3. Takashi likes reading printed books because he wants to ☐ 3 ☐ .

　① keep a lot of books in his room

　② look at a display for a long time

　③ read books outside of his house

　④ write things in them

One-Week Sale!

Simon's Sandwich Shop is going to have a sale for one week. You can buy our fresh sandwiches at a special price. Don't forget to tell your family and friends about this chance!

5 From Friday, May 26, to Thursday, June 1, every package of sandwiches at our shop is only $2 each. If you buy three packages of sandwiches, you will get one more for free. All drinks will be 10% off.

We will be open from 7 a.m. to 6 p.m. every day. We will not be closed any days during the sale.

10 For more information, please visit our website:
　　　　http://www.simonssandwichshop.com

(104 words)

Questions （目標1分30秒）

1. What is this notice about? 　1
　① A sale at a sandwich shop.
　② A sale at a supermarket.
　③ The new opening of a sandwich shop.
　④ The new opening of a supermarket.

2. People will get a free package of sandwiches 　2　.
　① if they buy three packages of sandwiches
　② if they buy ten packages of drinks
　③ if they go to the shop between May 26 and June 1
　④ if they go to the shop between 7 a.m. and 6 p.m.

3. If you want to know the address of the shop, you should 　3　.
　① ask your family or friends
　② check its website
　③ make a telephone call
　④ send an email to the shop

スピーキング・トレーナー
🔊 本文を音読しよう▮　　104語÷ 　　秒×60= 　　wpm

Lesson
4

対応試験

CEFR A1

共通テスト第1問A

目標1分40秒（60 wpm）
99語÷ ☐ 秒×60＝ ☐ wpm

You are a student at West High School.　You are reading a school newspaper and have found a notice written by Olivia, one of your English teachers.

Dear students at West High School,

North University is going to have an English speech contest for Japanese high school students on October 27.　The English teachers at our school are looking for some students who want to make a speech in the contest.　If you are interested in trying it, please make a short summary of your speech in about 30 words and hand it in to me by September 13.　You should speak about your dream for the future.　Your speech should be no longer than five minutes.　We are looking forward to hearing from you.

Olivia

(99 words)

Class　　No.　　Name

Questions （目標 1 分30秒）

1. On October 27, North University will ☐1☐.
   ① decide which essay is the best
   ② give a lecture about speeches to high school students
   ③ have a speech contest in Japanese
   ④ hold an event for high school students

2. If you want to enter the contest, you should hand in a summary of your speech to ☐2☐.
   ① a staff member of the school newspaper
   ② North University
   ③ Olivia
   ④ the principal of West High School

3. In the speech, you should talk about ☐3☐.
   ① how to make a speech for five minutes
   ② what you liked to do when you were a small child
   ③ what you want to become when you grow up
   ④ why you want to enter North University

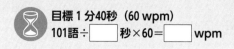

Hawaii is filled with natural places. Millions of tourists visit it every year. In Hawaii, they can enjoy not only its beautiful beaches but also its natural beauty in the mountains. Mauna Kea is about 4,200 meters high. It is the highest mountain in Hawaii. Many people climb it to see beautiful stars at night. Kilauea is also popular

5 because people can see an active volcano. Some people join a helicopter tour to see the mountain from the sky. There are a lot of forests in the mountain areas in Hawaii. Tourists can enjoy various activities such as hiking and bird-watching.

(101 words)

Class　　No.　　Name

Questions （目標１分30秒）

1. What is this passage mainly about? 　 1

　① How tourists enjoy activities in the forests in Hawaii.

　② How tourists enjoy looking at stars in Hawaii.

　③ How tourists enjoy the beaches in Hawaii.

　④ How tourists enjoy the mountains in Hawaii.

2. Why do many people climb Mauna Kea? 　 2

　① To enjoy bird-watching.

　② To see an active volcano.

　③ To see it from the sky.

　④ To see stars.

3. According to the passage, which of the following is true? 　 3

　① Hawaii is not famous for its beaches.

　② Kilauea is the highest mountain in Hawaii.

　③ People can go on a hike in the forests in Hawaii.

　④ There are more mountains in Hawaii now than before.

Lesson 6

対応試験

CEFR A1

英検® 3級 第3部A

目標2分 (65 wpm)
133語÷☐ 秒×60＝☐ wpm

Greentown High School Open House Day

Come to our open house day and find out about Greentown High School! In the morning, you can join one of the following three classes. You can do a science experiment with lemons and water guided by Mr. Wilson, have an omelet-cooking
5　lesson by Ms. Lee and the students from the cooking club, or have a Japanese art lesson by Mr. Ito.　After lunch, our class leaders will take you around our beautiful campus on a walking tour.

Date: Saturday, September 2

Time: 10:30 a.m. − 2:30 p.m.

Place: Greentown High School

10　You can have some sandwiches and a soft drink for free at lunchtime.
If you want to join this event, please visit our website and fill in the application form by the day before the event.

(133 words)

Class　　No.　　Name

Active
Practical Reading 導入編

Questions （目標1分30秒）

1. On the open house day, participants can join ⎡ 1 ⎤.
   ① a cooking lesson using lemons
   ② a lesson about making sandwiches with Ms. Lee
   ③ a science class by Mr. Wilson
   ④ an art lesson by students from the art club

2. How long is this event? ⎡ 2 ⎤
   ① Two hours.
   ② Three hours.
   ③ Four hours.
   ④ Five hours.

3. If you want to join this event, you should tell Greentown High School by ⎡ 3 ⎤.
   ① August 2
   ② August 26
   ③ September 1
   ④ September 2

You are in Sakuradai City on your bicycle.　You are checking the city's website on your smartphone to look for a place to park your bicycle.

Sakuradai City—Parking Lot Finder

The following map shows your location and bicycle parking lots around Sakuradai Station.　The parking lot numbers are circled.　The percentage shown under each circle shows how crowded the parking lot is.　When a parking lot is full of bicycles, you will see an "F" under the circle.　If there is a cross in the circle, the parking lot is closed for the day.

If you tap the circle, you will find the opening hours and the telephone number of each parking lot.　The percentage is updated every thirty minutes.　If you need the latest information, please call the bicycle parking lot.

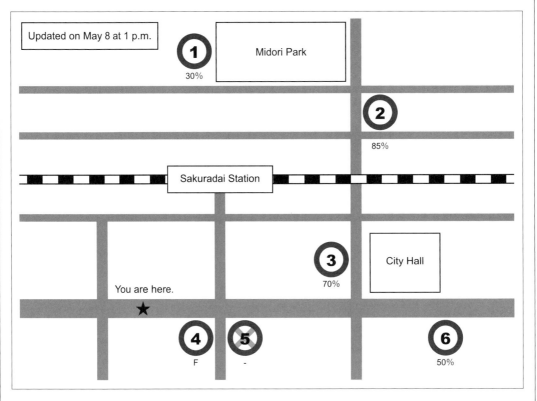

Note: Parking Lot 1 will be closed for 10 days, beginning May 9.

(148 words)

Class　No.　Name

Active
Practical Reading 導入編

Questions（目標 2 分）

1. Which of the following is true about the bicycle parking lot nearest to you now ?
   [1]
   ① It is closed.
   ② It is completely empty.
   ③ It is full.
   ④ It is half empty.

2. What information can you get by tapping the circle ? [2]
   ① How crowded the parking lot is.
   ② How to get to the parking lot's website.
   ③ When the parking lot is available.
   ④ When the parking lot was built.

3. Which is the nearest parking lot available to the people who will visit Midori Park on May 16 ? [3]
   ① Parking Lot 1.
   ② Parking Lot 2.
   ③ Parking Lot 3.
   ④ Parking Lot 4.

Cricket is one of the most popular sports around the world. In cricket, there are two teams in one game, and the players use bats and balls, so some people believe it is similar to baseball. However, there are several differences between the two sports. One great difference is the shape of the bats. The baseball bat is round, and a player can hit

5 the ball with any part of it. On the other hand, the cricket bat is flat, and a player can use only one side of it. The number of players is also different. There are nine players on one baseball team on the baseball field. On the other hand, eleven players are needed on a team to play cricket. If you are familiar with baseball, you will be surprised when you see a cricket player hit the ball in the center of the field. That

10 never happens in baseball games.

(154 words)

Class　　No.　　Name

Active
Practical Reading 導入編

Questions（目標１分30秒）

1. What is this passage mainly about? ☐ 1
   ① How cricket and baseball are similar.
   ② How cricket is different from baseball.
   ③ Why cricket has become popular around the world.
   ④ Why cricket bats are flat.

2. According to the passage, how many more players are there on a cricket team than on a baseball team? ☐ 2
   ① None.
   ② Two.
   ③ Nine.
   ④ Eleven.

3. According to the passage, which of the following is true? ☐ 3
   ① A baseball player hits the ball in the center of the field.
   ② A cricket player hits the ball with a flat bat.
   ③ Cricket is no longer popular around the world.
   ④ There are nine players on one cricket team.

You are reading an English newspaper.   You have found the article below.

Japanese mosquito net saves people from malaria.

Malaria is a serious disease.   Millions of people around the world suffer from this "devil's disease."   Every year, thousands of people die of it, and most of them are children.   People usually get malaria from mosquitoes.   Many people get it while they are sleeping because mosquitoes are active at night.

One Japanese company has been trying to solve this problem.   The company created a special mosquito net in 1994.   Since then, it has offered the nets to countries suffering from malaria, especially African countries.   The net is big enough for people to sleep under.   Mosquitoes can't get into it.   What is more, the net contains special chemicals which kill mosquitoes if they touch it.

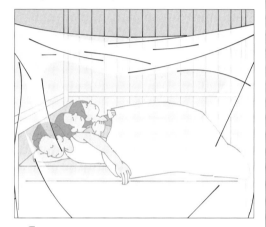

In Japan, many people used to sleep under a mosquito net called *kaya*.   It is no longer popular in Japan, but it still works overseas to save people's lives.

(150 words)

Questions （目標 1 分30秒）

1. Malaria ⬚ 1 ⬚.
   ① has disappeared in Africa
   ② has disappeared in Japan
   ③ kills only children
   ④ kills thousands of people every year

2. Many people get malaria while sleeping because ⬚ 2 ⬚.
   ① malaria is called the "devil's disease"
   ② mosquitoes never move at night
   ③ mosquitoes often fly at night
   ④ there is no mosquito net at night

3. The special chemicals in Japanese mosquito nets ⬚ 3 ⬚.
   ① help people to sleep well
   ② kill mosquitoes
   ③ make mosquitoes more active
   ④ make people resistant to malaria

You are planning to stay at a hotel and are looking for information on the Internet. You have found reviews for two hotels written by guests who have visited them.

Starlight Hotel

5

★★★★★ by Julia　(3 days ago)

Good location!　The hotel is in the city center.　It's a little far from the airport, but it's very close to Central Station. It was only a three-minute walk from it!

Hotel response:

> Julia, thank you for your comment.　We look forward to seeing you again.

---

10 ## Cedar Hotel

15

★★★★☆ by Wei　(5 days ago)

This small hotel is surrounded by forests.　I spent the weekend with my wife there, and we enjoyed a beautiful sunset in the mountains.　Nevertheless, we were disappointed that the restaurant was crowded in the morning.　Why don't you have some tables on the terrace, too?

Hotel response:

> Wei, thank you for your comment.　We are very sorry for our poor service in the morning.　Your comment will help us to make our service better.

20

(135 words)

Questions（目標2分）

1. Starlight Hotel will be a good choice if you are planning to ⬚ 1 ⬚.
   ① see a beautiful sunset
   ② stay near the airport
   ③ take a train to Central Station
   ④ walk in a forest

2. Cedar Hotel will be a good choice if you like ⬚ 2 ⬚.
   ① big hotels surrounded by forests
   ② eating on a terrace
   ③ the natural environment
   ④ walking around a city

3. In the review for Cedar Hotel, the guest wrote ⬚ 3 ⬚.
   ① advice for other guests
   ② advice for the hotel
   ③ an apology to the hotel
   ④ an apology to the other guests

4. According to the reviews, one **fact** about these hotels is that ⬚ 4 ⬚.
   ① Starlight Hotel is located beside the airport
   ② Starlight Hotel is the nearest hotel to Central Station
   ③ the restaurant at Cedar Hotel has a terrace
   ④ the service at Cedar Hotel is poor in the morning

スピーキング・トレーナー
本文を音読しよう⬚　135語÷⬚秒×60=⬚wpm

10-2

Lesson
11

対応試験

CEFR A1
GTEC® パートB

目標 1 分55秒 （75 wpm）
142語÷ □ 秒×60＝ □ wpm

https://wilsonhappytravel.com/bustour/

San Francisco Bus Tours

by Wilson Happy Travel

There are a lot of places to visit in San Francisco.
Join our bus tours and explore this exciting city!

For further information, write to info@wilsonhappytravel.com

Tour	Starting Time	Length (hours)	Meal	Price
Special Tour	10：30 a.m.	6	Lunch （Seafood）	$50
Deluxe Dinner Tour	5：30 p.m.	4	Dinner （French）	$60
Super Saver Tour	2：00 p.m.	3	None	$25
Museum Tour	9：00 a.m.	5	Lunch （Pasta）	$70

・ Click each tour title to check the places you can visit.

・ Click each price to check the prices for children under 12 years old.

・ An extra $5 will be added for each person for tours on Saturdays and Sundays.

・ Please make your reservation by email at least two days before the tour date.

・ Please arrive at the meeting place 20 minutes before the starting time of your tour.

Home ｜ News release ｜ Access ｜ Privacy ｜ Site map

（142 words）

Class　　No.　　Name

Questions（目標2分）

1. You want to have a meal in the evening on a bus tour.　Which tour is the best for you？　| 1 |
   ① Special Tour.
   ② Deluxe Dinner Tour.
   ③ Super Saver Tour.
   ④ Museum Tour.

2. You want to join the cheapest tour on the list with three friends on Sunday.　How much in total will you have to pay？　| 2 |
   ① $75.
   ② $90.
   ③ $100.
   ④ $120.

3. You want to join a tour with a seafood lunch.　By what time do you need to be at your meeting place？　| 3 |
   ① 9:00 a.m.
   ② 10:00 a.m.
   ③ 10:10 a.m.
   ④ 10:30 a.m.

4. You want to know whether you can visit Children's Creativity Museum on the Museum Tour.　According to the website, what should you do first？　| 4 |
   ① Call the tour company.
   ② Click "Museum Tour" on the list.
   ③ Click "$70" on the list.
   ④ Send an email to Wilson Happy Travel.

From: Akari Ito

To: Bella Scott

Date: Monday, March 24

Subject: *Hanami* Party

5 Hi, Bella!

I'm sorry you couldn't come to Mia's birthday party yesterday.　I heard you were sick in bed.　I hope you're all right now.　Mia and I are planning to have a *hanami* party in Midori Park this Sunday.　I'm sure the cherry blossoms will be at their best that day.　It's going to be crowded, though.　We hope you can join us.

10 Akari

From: Bella Scott

To: Akari Ito

Date: Tuesday, March 25

Subject: Re: *Hanami* Party

15 Hi, Akari!

I'm sorry I missed the birthday party.　I had a bad cold, but I'm fine now.　Thank you for inviting me to the *hanami* party.　I'd love to come!　I'll bring some fruits for you.　Also, I'll give Mia her birthday present on that day.　Let me know what time you are going to start the party.

20 Bella

(152 words)

Class　　No.　　Name

Questions （目標2分）

1. Why was Bella absent from Mia's birthday party?　| 1 |
   ① Because she got up late.
   ② Because she joined another party.
   ③ Because she was ill.
   ④ Because she went shopping.

2. When will the *hanami* party be held?　| 2 |
   ① March 23.
   ② March 24.
   ③ March 29.
   ④ March 30.

3. What will Midori Park be like this Sunday?　| 3 |
   ① All its cherry blossoms will have fallen.
   ② It will be crowded with sick people.
   ③ It will have a lot of beautiful cherry blossoms.
   ④ There will be few people there.

4. What information does Bella want?　| 4 |
   ① Advice for Mia's birthday present.
   ② Akari's favorite fruits.
   ③ The place for the *hanami* party.
   ④ The starting time of the *hanami* party.

Lesson
13

対応試験

CEFR A1
共通テスト第2問A

目標 1 分55秒 (80 wpm)
156語÷ □ 秒×60＝ □ wpm

You are going to make some Japanese sweets with your friends from abroad.　On a website, you have found a recipe for one popular sweet in Japan.

Sweet mochi is a traditional Japanese dessert.　It is very easy to make it at home. Here is a recipe.　Try it!

Sweet Mochi

—Ready in 50 minutes.

◆ Ingredients

 250g *mochi* flour

 220ml water

 150g sugar

 some cornstarch

◆ Instructions

1. Mix the *mochi* flour and the water in a bowl. Add more water if it is too dry.

2. Heat the dough in a steamer for 30 minutes.

3. Put the dough into a pot and cook it at medium heat.

4. Add the sugar little by little and mix well.

5. After all the sugar is dissolved, put the *mochi* onto a pan and dust it with cornstarch.

6. Shape it as you like with your hands.

◆ Review

Sophia (1 hour ago)
This is much easier than I thought!　I hear Japanese people like *mochi* with *anko* (sweet red bean paste) in it.　I'll be glad if you could show us how to make *anko*.

(156 words)

Class　　No.　　Name

Questions（目標2分）

1. This recipe will be a good choice if you want to ⬚ 1 ⬚ .
   ① eat a Japanese food for dessert
   ② make a Japanese-style drink
   ③ make a traditional American dish
   ④ prepare a dessert without using heat

2. According to this recipe, you can make the dessert in about ⬚ 2 ⬚ .
   ① 30 minutes
   ② 50 minutes
   ③ 1 hour
   ④ 1 hour and 30 minutes

3. If you want to make *sweet mochi* with this recipe, you will need ⬚ 3 ⬚ .
   ① a kitchen stove
   ② a knife
   ③ a refrigerator
   ④ an air conditioner

4. According to the website, one **fact** about this recipe is that ⬚ 4 ⬚ .
   ① a recipe for *anko* is going to be posted on the site within an hour
   ② it is easy to make *sweet mochi*
   ③ it is fun to cook with Japanese friends
   ④ it tells you to add the sugar slowly

Bayvale Aquarium's Weekend Evening Programs in October

Join us for our weekend evening programs at Bayvale Aquarium! Every weekend, we hold special events everyone will enjoy. While watching our beautiful sea creatures, you can enjoy a yoga lesson, a piano concert, a talk show and a Halloween
5 party. Check our website for more information.

Meeting place

The North Gate of Bayvale Aquarium
—Please arrive ten minutes before the event begins.

Events

Event	Date (In October)	Time
Yoga Lesson with Sea Life	Every Friday	6:00-7:30 p.m.
Piano Concert by the Water	Every Saturday except for the 31st	6:30-8:00 p.m.
Dr. Wilson's Talk Show	Every Sunday	5:50-7:00 p.m.
Halloween Party with Sharks	Oct. 31st (Saturday)	7:00-9:00 p.m.

Ticket fees

Member: $25, Non-member: $30 (for each event)

- Tickets must be purchased online in advance. Please show your e-ticket to the staff at the meeting place.
- All children under 16 must be accompanied by a parent or guardian.
- If you are interested in a membership, please check our website.

Bayvale Aquarium
www.bayvale-aquarium.com
4567-321-9999

(173 words)

Class No. Name

Active
Practical Reading 導入編

Questions （目標2分）

1. You want to join the yoga lesson. By what time do you need to be at the North Gate of Bayvale Aquarium? 　1

① 5:40 p.m.

② 5:50 p.m.

③ 6:00 p.m.

④ 6:10 p.m.

2. You want to join an event on Saturday, October 31. Which event(s) can you join? 　2

① Both the concert and the party.

② Both the yoga lesson and the talk show.

③ Only the concert.

④ Only the party.

3. Nobody in your family is a member of Bayvale Aquarium. How much will your family have to pay for three people to join one of the four events on the list? 　3

① $30.

② $75.

③ $90.

④ $120.

4. You are fifteen years old. What do you have to do if you want to join Dr. Wilson's Talk Show? 　4

① Become a member of Bayvale Aquarium.

② Check the information on Dr. Wilson's website.

③ Come to the aquarium with an adult.

④ Get permission from your parents to join the event.

スピーキング・トレーナー

本文を音読しよう□　173語÷□秒×60=□wpm

14-2

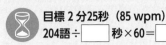

From: Kevin Davis

To: Takashi Imai

Date: Wednesday, July 2

Subject: My family

5　Hello, Takashi!

My name is Kevin Davis.　I'll be your host father when you stay with my family next month.　My wife Julie will be your host mother.　We have a son, Ryan.　He's been practicing *karate* for ten years.　He'll enter high school next September. Also, we have a daughter, Olivia.　She is only eight years old.　She loves music.

10　We're looking forward to seeing you here in Florida.

Julie and I are planning to take you to an arena to watch a basketball game during your stay.　Are you interested in basketball?　Is there anything you want to do here?

Best regards,

15　Kevin

From: Takashi Imai

To: Kevin Davis

Date: Thursday, July 3

Subject: Greetings from Japan

20　Hello, Mr. Davis!

Thank you for your kind message.　It'll be the first time for me to go abroad.　I'm really excited to stay with you in Florida.　I'm on the basketball team in my school, so I'm very interested in watching a basketball game in the U.S.!　I also like swimming.　If it's no problem for you, I'd like to go swimming in the sea with your

25　family.

Sincerely,

Takashi Imai

(204 words)

Class　　No.　　Name

Active
Practical Reading 導入編

Questions （目標 2 分）

1. When is Takashi going to stay with Kevin's family?　 1

　① In June.

　② In July.

　③ In August.

　④ In September.

2. Kevin and Julie are planning to　 2 　.

　① go to a basketball game

　② go to a high school

　③ play basketball

　④ swim in the sea

3. How many times has Takashi been to foreign countries?　 3

　① Never.

　② Once.

　③ Twice.

　④ Three times.

4. Which club activity does Takashi do at school?　 4

　① Basketball.

　② *Karate*.

　③ Music.

　④ Swimming.

You are planning to travel around Dubai in the Middle East and you are looking for information on the Internet.　You have found a tour schedule and reviews for a tour.

Tour Schedule for 4 Days in Dubai ($2,300)

Day	Activity	Details	Meal
Day 1	Arrival in Dubai　STAY　HOTEL	Arrive at Dubai International Airport and transfer to the hotel.　Check in at the hotel in Dubai and have an Arabian dinner at the restaurant in the hotel.	B : ✈ L : ✕ D : 🍖
Day 2	Dubai City Tour and Dinner Cruise　STAY　HOTEL	Have breakfast at the hotel and leave for the Dubai City Tour.　The tour includes entrance fees to Dubai Museum, Jumeirah Mosque and Burj Khalifa.　Lunch is not included in the tour.　In the evening, have a French dinner on a cruise.	B : 🍳 L : ✕ D : 🍽
Day 3	Free Day (Optional Tour)　STAY　HOTEL	Have breakfast at the hotel and enjoy the day on your own.　You can join the optional Evening Desert Tour starting at 3 p.m.　The tour includes a drive by car in the desert, a camel ride, and a barbecue dinner.　The tour ends at 9 p.m.	B : 🍳 L : ✕ D : 🍽
Day 4	Departure from Dubai　STAY　✈	Have breakfast at the hotel.　Check out of the hotel and transfer to Dubai International Airport.	B : 🍳 L : ✕ D : ✈

★★★★★ by Louise （August 30）

You MUST join the optional tour!　It was amazing for me to ride a camel in the desert.　But be careful.　It's very hot in the desert in summer!

★★★★☆ by Kazuya （September 8）

I enjoyed Dubai on this tour.　I liked the Arabian food, so I wanted to have an Arabian dinner again on the second evening.　Also, I thought the tour was a little expensive.

(239 words)

Class　　No.　　Name

Active
Practical Reading 導入編

Questions （目標2分）

1. This four-day tour will be a good choice if you want to ☐ 1 ☐.
   ① have dinner at the hotel every evening
   ② have lunch as you like
   ③ ride a camel in the morning
   ④ take a train in Dubai

2. You can have dinner on a ship on ☐ 2 ☐.
   ① the first day
   ② the second day
   ③ the third day
   ④ the fourth day

3. One traveler on this tour complains about ☐ 3 ☐.
   ① the Arabian food
   ② the camel ride
   ③ the climate in the city
   ④ the tour fee

4. According to the schedule and the reviews, one **opinion** about the optional tour is that
   ☐ 4 ☐.
   ① it ends at 9 p.m. on the third day
   ② it is a good idea to join it
   ③ people must not join it in summer
   ④ the barbecue dinner on it is very nice

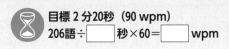

You have found the following story in a blog written by Sophia, an American high school girl.

Outside a Library

Sunday, October 23

5　This morning, I was really excited to visit a library in my town because I was going to borrow a new novel written by my favorite writer, Michael Orwell.　I left home at 8:45 and rode my bicycle for fifteen minutes.　I arrived at the library and found that something was strange.　There was nobody around there.　"The library should be open by now on Sunday," I thought.　At the entrance, I found a sign

10　saying, "Closed for Building Maintenance."

I felt disappointed and stood there for a while.　I didn't know what to do instead. Then, I saw an elderly woman approaching the library.　"Oh, dear.　I didn't know it's closed," she said.　"Me, neither.　Disappointing, isn't it?" I asked.　"Not really. That's life.　Life has ups and downs," she replied with a smile.　Then, she started

15　talking about her life full of ups and downs.　Her life story was like an exciting novel.　Finally, she said, "I'm a big fan of Michael Orwell."　I was surprised and happy to hear that.

I went back home.　I took out one of my old books by Michael Orwell from my bookshelf.　While reading it, I remembered the woman's happy smile.

(206 words)

Class　　No.　　Name

Questions （目標2分）

1. Sophia arrived at the library at ⬚ 1 ⬚.

　① 8：45

　② 8：50

　③ 8：55

　④ 9：00

2. The library was closed because ⬚ 2 ⬚.

　① its condition was being checked

　② nobody was around there

　③ some books by Michael Orwell had been lost

　④ there were too many bicycles around the building

3. At the entrance, the elderly woman was feeling ⬚ 3 ⬚.

　① angry

　② disappointed

　③ positive

　④ sad

4. At home, Sophia read ⬚ 4 ⬚.

　① a book about a happy smile

　② a book from the library

　③ a book she had

　④ a book the elderly woman had given her

Lesson

18

対応試験

GTEC® パートC
英検® 3級 第3部C

目標 2分10秒 (90 wpm)
205語÷□秒×60=□wpm

CEFR A1

Dogs are very smart animals. They can learn many kinds of tricks and commands from their owners. They can know when their owners are happy or angry with them. For these reasons, dogs are often called "man's best friend."

Dogs are so smart that they can learn how to control people in surprising ways. One example is a fake sickness. When they feel lonely, some dogs will pretend to be sick in front of their owners. There are a lot of reports about pet dogs coughing or making a strange noise even though they are healthy. It is also reported that they tend to stop doing it when their owners begin to talk or stay with them. This means that they fake sickness because they want to get attention from their owners.

Do dogs really know how to fake sickness? The answer is no. They just learn that they can get a good result for them when they act sick. So it is important for owners not to punish the behavior of a fake sickness. Owners should ignore dogs showing a fake sickness, and they should give dogs a lot of love and attention when they do not show the signs of a fake sickness.

(205 words)

Class　　No.　　Name

Active
Practical Reading 導入編

Questions （目標 2 分）

1. What is this passage mainly about? 　 1

　① How to treat a pet dog when it is sick.

　② What we know about dogs' fake sicknesses.

　③ When dogs stop showing the signs of a fake sickness.

　④ Why people call dogs "man's best friend."

2. Which of the following proves that dogs are smart? 　 2

　① Dogs can control their owners by tricks and commands.

　② Dogs can give their owners love and attention.

　③ Dogs can know their owners' emotions.

　④ Dogs can understand the meaning of "man's best friend."

3. Why do dogs show a fake sickness? 　 3

　① They want their owners to care for them.

　② They want their owners to ignore them.

　③ They want their owners to notice their real sickness.

　④ They want their owners to teach some tricks to them.

4. According to the passage, which of the following is the best way to treat dogs showing a fake sickness? 　 4

　① To give them attention.

　② To leave them alone.

　③ To punish them.

　④ To take them to an animal hospital.

You have found the following story in a blog written by Brendan, a university student studying in Japan.

Japanese Convenience Stores
Wednesday, June 1

5 　I'm Brendan from Australia. I've been here in Japan for three years studying Japanese culture at university. In Japan, convenience stores are everywhere. Even in small convenience stores in the countryside, there is everything you need for daily life. You can find food, drinks, magazines and even ATM machines! Surprisingly, most of them open for 24 hours! They are so convenient that going to
10 them is an important part of my life in Japan.

　These days, more and more Japanese people are considering the following question: Do convenience stores have to open for 24 hours? Some people believe that there are some bad points in opening stores for 24 hours. They say that it is not good for workers' health to work at night very often. Store owners find it hard
15 to find people who want to work at night. They also say that opening stores at night wastes energy, such as electricity. Others believe that there are still good points in keeping stores open 24 hours. They say that it is necessary for people to have chances to buy things at any time. Also, they say that closing stores at night will decrease their profits.
20 　In my view, it is important for each store to have the right to choose whether it will stay open for 24 hours or not. What do you think?

(231 words)

Questions （目標 2 分）

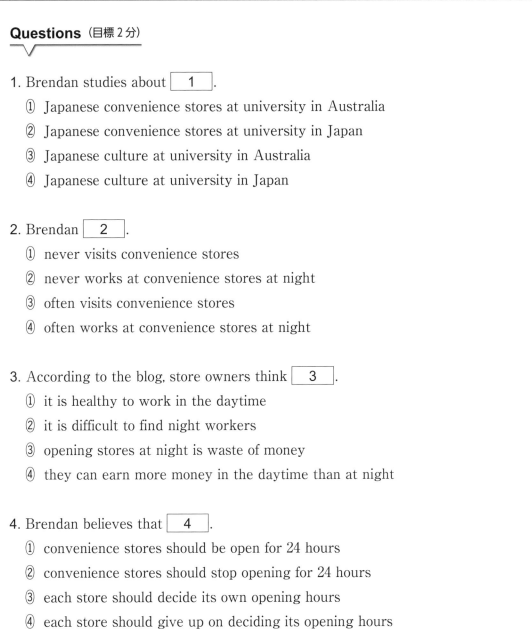

1. Brendan studies about [1].
   ① Japanese convenience stores at university in Australia
   ② Japanese convenience stores at university in Japan
   ③ Japanese culture at university in Australia
   ④ Japanese culture at university in Japan

2. Brendan [2].
   ① never visits convenience stores
   ② never works at convenience stores at night
   ③ often visits convenience stores
   ④ often works at convenience stores at night

3. According to the blog, store owners think [3].
   ① it is healthy to work in the daytime
   ② it is difficult to find night workers
   ③ opening stores at night is waste of money
   ④ they can earn more money in the daytime than at night

4. Brendan believes that [4].
   ① convenience stores should be open for 24 hours
   ② convenience stores should stop opening for 24 hours
   ③ each store should decide its own opening hours
   ④ each store should give up on deciding its opening hours

Lesson
20

対応試験 GTEC® パートC
英検® 3級 第3部C

CEFR A1

目標 2 分30秒 (90 wpm)
225語÷ [　] 秒×60= [　] wpm

Erasers are useful. They are also called "rubbers" in some countries. They can remove pencil marks from paper. If you have this small useful item, you don't have to be afraid of making mistakes when you write or draw something. Do you know how they were first invented and how they have evolved since then?

⁵ In the middle of the 16th century, a good-quality material for pencils was discovered in England. People started making pencils and the products spread all over Europe. At that time, people used pieces of bread for erasing their writing and drawings. In 1770, Edward Nairne, an English engineer, accidentally picked up a piece of rubber instead of bread and discovered that rubber can erase pencil marks. He started selling ¹⁰ rubber erasers, and this became a great success. However, there were some problems with this kind of eraser. They easily broke into small pieces when they were used. Also, they melted easily and smelled bad when it was hot.

In 1839, an American inventor named Charles Goodyear invented a way to make rubber last longer. This invention made rubber erasers harder to break. Thanks to ¹⁵ this invention, they became very popular all over the world.

Today we have many kinds of erasers with different shapes, sizes and materials. Isn't it interesting to imagine what they will be like in the future?

(225 words)

Class　　No.　　Name

Active
Practical Reading 導入編

Questions （目標2分）

1. What is this passage mainly about? 　1
   ① How people will invent erasers in the future.
   ② The history of erasers.
   ③ The relationship between erasers and bread.
   ④ Ways to succeed in selling products.

2. What was found in England in the middle of the 16th century? 　2
   ① A good substance for making erasers.
   ② A good substance for making pencils.
   ③ Bread for erasing pencil marks.
   ④ Rubber for erasing pencil marks.

3. What did Edward Nairne do? 　3
   ① He caused a serious accident.
   ② He discovered that bread can erase pencil markings.
   ③ He invented a way to make rubber last longer.
   ④ He sold erasers made of rubber.

4. What happened after Charles Goodyear's invention? 　4
   ① Goodyear's erasers melted and smelled bad.
   ② People all over the world started to use erasers.
   ③ People imagined what erasers would be like in the future.
   ④ Rubber erasers became easier to break into small pieces.

You have found the following story in a blog written by a Canadian man named Jason Cote.

Winter in Canada
Friday, December 1

5   It's the beginning of December. It's very cold here in Montreal, Canada. The temperature has fallen to −15℃! It's five degrees lower than yesterday. It's snowing a lot. Clearing the snow is hard work. The nights are long, and the days are short. Winter is really harsh here.

   I've been living in Montreal for 35 years, which is all my life. When I was a child,
10 my parents often took me to a ski course near my house. It was only a twenty-minute drive from the center of Montreal. It was a lot of fun, and I loved winter. As I grew older, I came to dislike cold temperatures and the short days in winter, and I became less interested in skiing. I stopped skiing.

   Soon after I got married five years ago, my wife asked me to go skiing with her. I
15 didn't feel like going at first, but finally, I accepted her invitation. While I was driving the car, she was excited. I wasn't so much. We got to the ski course I used to visit with my parents. Once I started skiing, I remembered my childhood days. Though I'd stopped skiing for years, I soon remembered how to ski. It was a lot of fun. Since then, I've been to dozens of ski courses around Canada.

20   Now I love Canadian winter as much as I did when I was a child. I'm thankful to my wife, who reminded me of my passion in my childhood.

(254 words)

Class   No.   Name

Active
Practical Reading 導入編

Questions （目標 2 分）

1. According to Jason, the temperature on November 30 was ⬚ 1 ⬚ .

   ① 5℃

   ② –5℃

   ③ –10℃

   ④ –20℃

2. When he was a child, Jason ⬚ 2 ⬚ .

   ① disliked cold temperatures in winter

   ② stopped skiing

   ③ went skiing around Canada with his parents

   ④ went to a ski course near his house

3. When he was driving to the ski course, Jason felt ⬚ 3 ⬚ .

   ① angry

   ② excited

   ③ thankful

   ④ uninterested

4. Jason thanks his wife because ⬚ 4 ⬚ .

   ① she drove him to his favorite ski course

   ② she has skied with him around Canada

   ③ she made him remember his childhood days

   ④ she taught him how to ski

Lesson
22

対応試験

CEFR A1
GTEC® パートC
英検® 3 級 第 3 部 C

目標 2 分50秒 （90 wpm）
250語÷ ☐ 秒×60= ☐ wpm

The French Language

The French language is the official language of France. It is also spoken in many other areas, such as Switzerland, Belgium, Luxembourg, Quebec in Canada and some countries in Africa. More than 200 million people speak it as a first or second language
5 around the world. It is one of the official languages of the United Nations and some other international organizations. Therefore, French is thought to be one of the world's major languages, in addition to English.

Most languages in the world belong to a language group. There are many similarities between the languages in one group. French is a member of the Romance
10 group of languages. You will notice many similarities between French, Spanish, Italian and Portuguese because they are all Romance languages.

In about the 8th century, people in northern France started to use Old French, which was similar to Latin. In 1066, the ruler of Normandy, which is an area in northern France, conquered England. This event is now known as the Norman Conquest. It
15 changed the English language. French was used in England for writing for about 200 years afterward. In this period, English acquired many new words from French. In today's English, it is easy to find such words as "table," "beef," "nice" and so on. For this reason, French is easier to learn for people who can speak English.

The French language has a close historical relationship with English and plays an
20 important role as a language for global communication.

(250 words)

Class   No.   Name

Questions（目標2分）

1. The official languages of the United Nations include ▢ 1 ▢ .

　① French

　② Italian

　③ Latin

　④ Portuguese

2. Why are there many similarities between French, Spanish, Italian and Portuguese?
　▢ 2 ▢

　① They are official languages of France.

　② They are spoken all over the world.

　③ They are used in romantic stories.

　④ They belong to the same language group.

3. What happened in 1066? ▢ 3 ▢

　① A ruler of England conquered Normandy.

　② England was invaded by the ruler of a part of France.

　③ People started to use Old French.

　④ The French language was totally changed.

4. Why is it easier for English speakers to learn French? ▢ 4 ▢

　① A lot of English words came from French.

　② Both French and English play an important role in global communication.

　③ England has a close historical relationship with France.

　④ French people have used English for about 200 years.